Growing Up and Looking Out

GROWING UP
and
LOOKING OUT

My Life from Laguna
Pueblo to Albuquerque
and
Tales
My
Grandmother Told Me
and Being Laguna

Katherine Augustine

SUNSTONE
PRESS

SANTA FE

Sunstone books may be purchased for educational, business, or sales promotional use.
For information please write: Special Markets Department, Sunstone Press,
P.O. Box 2321, Santa Fe, New Mexico 87504-2321.

Book and cover design › Vicki Ahl
Body typeface › Adobe Garamond Pro
Printed on acid-free paper
∞
eBook 978-1-61139-514-3

Library of Congress Cataloging-in-Publication Data

ON FILE

SUNSTONE PRESS IS COMMITTED TO MINIMIZING OUR ENVIRONMENTAL IMPACT ON THE PLANET. THE PAPER USED IN THIS BOOK IS FROM
RESPONSIBLY MANAGED FORESTS. OUR PRINTER HAS RECEIVED CHAIN OF CUSTODY (COC) CERTIFICATION FROM: THE FOREST STEWARDSHIP
COUNCIL™ (FSC®), PROGRAMME FOR THE ENDORSEMENT OF FOREST CERTIFICATION™ (PEFC™), AND THE SUSTAINABLE FORESTRY INITIATIVE® (SFI®).
THE FSC® COUNCIL IS A NON-PROFIT ORGANIZATION, PROMOTING THE ENVIRONMENTALLY APPROPRIATE, SOCIALLY BENEFICIAL AND
ECONOMICALLY VIABLE MANAGEMENT OF THE WORLD'S FORESTS. FSC® CERTIFICATION IS RECOGNIZED INTERNATIONALLY AS A
RIGOROUS ENVIRONMENTAL AND SOCIAL STANDARD FOR RESPONSIBLE FOREST MANAGEMENT.

WWW.SUNSTONEPRESS.COM
SUNSTONE PRESS / POST OFFICE BOX 2321 / SANTA FE, NM 87504-2321 /USA
(505) 988-4418 / ORDERS ONLY (800) 243-5644 / FAX (505) 988-1025

To my beloved grandmother, Reyes Paisano.

Contents

Preface and Acknowledgement

Katherine Augustine is an extraordinary person. She grew up on the Laguna Indian Reservation in the 1930s and was raised by a beloved grandmother. In the 1940s she lived in a boxcar in Gallup with her parents and five siblings. Her father worked for the railroad and during a summer vacation from the Albuquerque Indian Boarding School she worked as a Harvey Girl. Following graduation from high school she went to nursing school in Ganado, Arizona, became a registered nurse, and had a long career as a nurse in Albuquerque. She has won numerous service awards, served on numerous community boards, has been and is a volunteer for a variety of community organizations.

For over thirty years she wrote stories about her life and observations of growing up at Laguna Pueblo, along with articles on current events for several publications. These included the Indian Pueblo Cultural Center newsletter *Pueblo Horizons*, a column for the now defunct evening newspaper the *Albuquerque Tribune*, articles for the *Albuquerque Laguna Colony Newsletter*, and *Round the Roundhouse*, the New Mexico State Employees newsletter.

This book tells Katherine's story in her own words. It is drawn entirely from a selection of her writings in various publications. Copies of all of her writings are available to the public at the New Mexico State Archives in Santa Fe, New Mexico and at the Center For Southwest Research, University of New Mexico as well as the Archives of the Indian Pueblo Cultural Center (IPCC), in Albuquerque, New Mexico.

The book is in two parts. The first, "My Life From Laguna Pueblo to Albuquerque" is Katherine's autobiography from her childhood to the start of her nursing career. The second, "Tales My Grandmother Told Me and Being Laguna" is a collection of Laguna Pueblo stories she learned as a child and observations of feast days and public ceremonies.

Photographs in the first section are from Katherine's family album, while images illustrating stories from Laguna Pueblo are derived from photographs of prehistoric art in the collection of Paul R. Secord.

—Paul R. Secord, Albuquerque, New Mexico 2017

My Life From Laguna Pueblo to Albuquerque

*T*his is an autobiography that I wrote in a series of newspaper articles over a number of years. While for most of my life I have been a practicing nurse, active community volunteer, and traveled the world, I think my growing up on Laguna Pueblo, going to the Albuquerque Indian School, having a brief job as a Harvey Girl, and becoming a nurse will be of most interest to you.

We're So Close, and Yet, the History Hurts

*L*et me tell you a little bit about myself.

My name before I married was Katherine Acoya. The name Acoya in the Keres language means earring. Keres is the language I speak.

Before my paternal grandfather went to Carlisle Indian School in Pennsylvania in 1881 at the age of twelve he was Shu-we-mei Oh-ku-ya-mei, meaning turquoise earring. When he returned home four years later he was Henry Acoya. He had refused the surname Analla, which was given to his brothers Fred and Thomas, who went with him to the boarding school.

I was born on the Laguna reservation some sixty-eight years ago. I don't mind telling you my age—the eldest of eight children. I was raised by my grandparents in the small village of Paguate, ten miles north of the mother village of Laguna Pueblo.

At twelve years old, I was sent to the Albuquerque Indian School to pursue studies in English, math, history, geography and mostly home economics for five years.

At age seventeen, I entered nurse's training in Arizona and, upon graduation in 1950, I worked continuously in that profession; twenty-nine years at the Presbyterian Hospital in a supervisory position, five years at the Women's and Children's Hospital and nine years with the Indian Health Service. I retired five years ago and do volunteer work here at the Indian Pueblo Culture Center. Also, I serve on the Health Board of the Acoma-Canoncito-Laguna Hospital, where I once worked as a staff nurse.

I am honored to be representing my tribe in that capacity.

My nursing career took me to Siberia, Central Asia, Moscow, Lithuania and China to teach intravenous-therapy nursing through the People to People Ambassador Program. I have traveled with the Friendship Force and the Albuquerque Sister Cities Foundation as an ambassador to Australia, New Zealand, Japan, South Korea, the Philippines and a great part of east and west Europe.

So, what does my history have to do with the proposed monument in Tiguex Park honoring Don Juan de Onate, who led the Spanish colonization of New Mexico four hundred years ago?

I am constantly perplexed about the "controversy" the newspapers and television say exists in the upcoming celebration of the Cuarto Centenario.

I am here today representing myself I cannot tell you if or how the monument debate has divided the Hispanics and the Native Americans in this state. I can only give you my personal perspective.

I have two great grandchildren who are one eighth Acoma, one eighth Laguna and three quarters Hispanic. Do I love them less than the great grandchild who is one half Sac and Fox, one quarter Creek of the Oklahoma tribes and one eighth Acoma, one eighth Laguna Pueblo tribes? I don't think so. I love them all equally.

If today they were old enough to comprehend the present debate going on, would I be so crass as to say to my Hispanic great grand children: "Your Spanish ancestors were very cruel people, they killed my Indian people," or "the Indians had good cause to kill the Spaniards"?

On the other hand, do I just forget the stories my grandparents told me about the events that took place in the late 1800s, when the Indian schools were run by the Protestant missionaries who tried to keep the Native Americans from practicing their "pagan religion"? That same religion which is alive and well today is used in our daily lives.

The Spanish Catholic priests went into our villages and beat the Pueblo people to get them to submit to praying for their saints. Catholicism has survived in the Pueblos, as you can tell by the many churches that stand in even the smallest villages on the reservations and by the feast day celebrations in honor of the saints.

A majority of Pueblo people have Spanish surnames and have adopted parts of that language into their own native tongues.

Because I am an urban Indian, I have friends who come from various cultures. I live in the North Valley of Albuquerque, which was at one time part of the Elena Gallegos grant and was in fact the village of Los Griegos in 1875–1930. My neighbors are Hispanic folks whose families built some of the homes they still live in today.

That area of town was also occupied by the Pueblo Indians thousands of years ago when they lived in pit houses along the Rio Grande. Today, whenever an excavation takes place to build a house foundation, Pueblo pottery shards and ruins surface, bringing back history showing that our ancestor's spirits are still there.

I remember a fervent episode that occurred between two great friends, one my son Don and the other Peter O. Griego III. They were about fourteen or fifteen when they were students at Valley High School.

One day Peter said to Don, "You know that my street, Griegos Road, was named after my great-grandfather."

To this, Don replied: "Of course, that happened after your people took the land away from mine."

I think it was two years later that Peter died in a motorcycle accident, and his family and mine were grieving together.

Then when I was a small child in Paguate, living there with my grandparents, we had neighbors to the north of the village. They were the Ka-chu-tda, the Spanish who lived in three little villages—Seboyeta, Bibo and Moquino.

My grandparents both spoke Spanish, and we had friends in all three places. We went to their homes, they came to ours, we ate their food, they ate ours, and we traded chickens and fruit. We had many good times together. These are some of the treasured memories from my past.

So back to 1598, when Don Juan de Onate led an expedition of Spanish colonists to our Pueblos and brutalized our people and back to the Pueblo Revolt of 1680 when the Spaniards were chased out of New Mexico. Where does that leave me, or what does it lead me to?

In my neighborhood of Hispanic and Anglo people, we are all fighting for the same things necessary to maintain a good quality place to live. We have Columbus Park where our children and grandchildren play; we have Anderson Fields with one hundred year old cottonwood trees and alfalfa fields. Ditches still exist in that part of town, and ducks swim in those waterways from March to November.

We lost part of our country like atmosphere to the Montano Bridge. We fought long and hard against the construction, my Hispanic and Anglo neighbors and I. These are the things that hold us together in our daily lives.

I am neither Catholic nor Protestant, but I believe in my native teachings that all things are sacred, that we are all one people.

At this time I do not know if or how many of the planned Cuarto Centenario events I will attend.

I do know one thing of extreme interest to me and much concern: that some history books written today reflect inaccurate accounts pertaining to the Native Americans and some do not, and that this history be taught in each and every classroom in America.

—*Albuquerque Tribune: Insight & Opinion*, May 12, 1998.
From April 4th panel discussion on celebrations of
four hundred years of Spanish influence in New Mexico.

**My official photograph at the
Albuquerque Convention Center
Hall of Fame, 2009.**

Indian "Education" Meant Changing Names

Shu-we-mei O-ku-ya-me was my paternal grandfather's name before he went to Carlisle Indian School in Pennsylvania in 1881. His name, meaning "turquoise earring" in the Keres language, has been shortened to "Acoya."

Grandfather Henry Acoya was born about 1869, the second of eight children his father Harumie, and his wife, whose name I do not know, had. All four boys and four girls were born on the Laguna Pueblo forty-five miles west of Albuquerque.

The eight children grew up learning the tribal traditions and the language spoken by their people. The boys worked with their father tilling the fields, planting, irrigating and harvesting the crops. The girls assisted their mother with the younger children and household chores. Harumie and his wife felt fortunate to have so many children in their home.

Fortunate, that is, until one day, when a United States government agent came to their door and took away O'ku-ya-me, who was twelve, and his brothers Sea-sin, ten, and Secu-real, six. The year was 1881, two years after the railroad came through the Pueblo of Laguna.

The three brothers, frightened, clung to each other and cried as the great iron horse pulled away from their homeland to take them 2,000 miles east to become educated. Their parents, who were heartbroken; did not know where they were being taken, nor did they know if they would see them again.

In the 1800s, Indian schools were run by missionaries; Protestants, who were trying to keep the Indians from practicing their "pagan religion," and Catholics, who were beating them to get them to submit to praying to the saints.

Then, about 1870, one hundred seventy years later Congress appropriated $100,000 for Indian education and authorized extension of federal services to the Pueblo Indians. By then, military campaigns against all Indians had stopped and the idea for Indian boarding schools was conceived.

U.S. Army Officer Richard Henry Pratt, then in charge of Plains Indian prisoners at Fort Marion; Fla. confirmed success in the use of discipline to control the Indians. He found it effective also in teaching them the English language. He truly believed that educating Indian people in a military type school would conform them to the Anglo American way of life. With this concept, the Carlisle Indian School was born in 1879.

The school, in an abandoned military post and its barracks in Pennsylvania, housed Indian children gathered from throughout the United States. Students wore uniforms and followed military discipline. Only English was spoken. Half a day was spent in learning the language, reading, writing and arithmetic. The rest of the day was spent in industrial or vocational training, tailoring, blacksmithing or farming for the boys, and sewing, ironing, cooking and laundering for' girls.

An "outing program" during the summer placed children with white families to accustom them to non-Indian life. Out of loneliness, some students tried to run away. When caught, they were punished by being, whipped or chained to an iron pole. Some of them never returned home. Either they died from severe punishment or some disease.

In 1885, four years after grandfather was taken away, he was allowed to return home. He could speak English, and he had learned, better ways to farm. His long, black hair was replaced by a haircut, cropped close to his scalp. He wore strange clothing, brown serge pants with a jacket that matched and a military hat. He did now know what to make of his former surroundings when he arrived at the train station at Laguna.   The houses looked very small to him. His parents' and siblings had moved to a village called Seama, several miles from where he was born.

Something else happened to him at Carlisle Indian School. He was no longer Shu-we-mei Osku-ya-me. He was now Henry Acoya, an "educated' man who had almost a European name, except that he did not allow the authorities to change this part of him.

They wanted him to be Henry "Analla," but he refused, finally compromising on the name Acoya for convenience of pronunciation and writing. His brother Sea-Sin became Fred Analla, and Se-cu-real was known as Thomas Analla.

At age twenty-four, grandfather married my grandmother, Maria, who was twenty-two. They had eight children, five boys and three girls, two of whom, a boy and a girl, died in infancy. My dad, Benjamin, married my mom, Howy Paisano, and they also had eight of us, six boys and two girls. And so the name Acoya was carried from 1881 into the new millennium.

—*Albuquerque Tribune*, January 16, 2000.

My parents Bennie and Howye.

A Morn, Moment with Grandmother

*I*t was moderately cool that long ago autumn morning, with a slight breeze whispering through the old apple tree in front of our house in Paguate on Laguna Pueblo.

"It will warm up soon," Grandmother promised, as we walked toward the wooden bench next to the barren tree. The fruit it had produced, the San Juan apple, was a sweet little golf ball sized apple that ripened on June 24, that saint's day.

My maternal grandmother, Reyes Paisano, raised me from a small child and taught me many cultural aspects of Pueblo life, including tribal traditions and the Keres language. She took me with her while doing chores, except when she was performing midwife duties, and most of those took place at night.

Her long, shiny, black hair was rolled up and tied at the back of her head with a small red and white woven hair tie. Over her homemade print dress, she wore the black manta with a red, green and black sash that Grandfather had made around her waist. She wore brown cotton stockings held in place by two elastic bands above the knees. Her well-worn brown shoes were dusty from walking about the gardens and orchards at this time of year. Dressing in the morning was as much a ritual for her as praying and scattering cornmeal at sunrise.

On that fall day in 1935, when I was about six years old, it was our job to husk the corn that lay in a huge pile next to the apple tree. The husks, when removed, revealed cobs of beautiful , shades of yellow, orange, red, purple and blue. The white ones were never too exciting, but they were the most important ones in the bunch because they provided the sacred cornmeal used in blessing ceremonies.

"Dwa-oh (Granddaughter), save the large husks for wrapping the tamales," Grandmother instructed. "The blue corn will go in the tub." She gestured with a nod of her head to the left. Then, waving her brown, wrinkled hand outward to the right, she continued, "The white ones go on the canvas, and the rest will be taken to the barn to store for the animals to eat in the winter time."

Grandmother brought out an old chair that no longer had a back, while I perched on the bench. As we husked, the corn, she told me a story I had never heard before:

"It was this time of the year that the Apaches killed my father," she stated with sadness in her voice. "That was a long, long time ago, when the Apaches and Navajos were raiding our pueblos.

My father had a cornfield and tended to it, much as your grandfather does today. Everyone was still living in Old Laguna Village, before there were too many people and they had to leave to the other villages, so they could have space to farm.

"My two sisters were quite young then, and I was waiting to be born, my parents hoping that I would be a boy to help father with his tasks.

"It was evening on that particular day, when my father had made piles of corn in the field to be picked up the next day with a wagon, when the three Red Shirts (called that because they wore red shirts) appeared from nowhere. They shot him with an arrow in the abdomen and loaded their horses with all the corn they could carry, and left.

"With the arrow impaled in him, he walked home, stopping every little while to catch his breath. He made his way home, arriving soon after my birth." My mother and other relatives told me that he lived long enough to see me as a newborn baby. She ended the narration; wiping away tears with her apron.

No one really knew how old Grandmother was when she died in 1950, but it was in the 1850s when the Apaches and Navajos were raiding. The Navajos were taken to Fort Sumner in 1864, but the Apaches continued to attack for several more years.

—*Albuquerque Tribune*, October 2003.

Growing Up in a Time of Storytelling, Wagons, Feasts

*I*t was August, 1937. I was eight years old, living with Grandmother in Paguate, about ten miles north of Laguna Pueblo and five miles south of the Spanish villages of Bibo, Seboyeta and Moquino. Keres was the language I spoke.

We lived in a five-room stone and mud house that my grandfather built many years before I was born. I think it may have been even older than my mother, who was thirty years old at that time. I was born in this house on September 30, 1929. Grandmother, who was a midwife, attended my birth.

Grandpa lived with us until he died in 1939. I knew that his death was imminent, because he called my mother and my aunt to his bedside the night before he went to the Spirit World. He gave them advice on how to raise their children and let them know about the land that would be theirs. He was buried in a casket built of wood and covered with a black cloth. My father had spent a whole day making it.

I cried for many days after he left us, but Grandmother said I should not be sad, for his spirit would always be in out midst.

I remember him as a tall, strong man who wore a red, printed bandana around his head to keep his shoulder length black hair in place. He wore Levis pants topped with a shirt made by Grandmother. He liked wearing high-top, black and white tennis shoes. They felt like "wearing moccasins," he said.

In the wintertime, Grandpa told my cousins and me many stories of Spiderwoman and the Twin Boy Heroes.

This storytelling took place in the middle room of our house, which contained a corner fireplace. We sat on the floor on sheepskins placed on top of a large Navajo rug, eating pinions or parched corn as we listened, intently at first, then gradually drifted off to sleep induced from the crackling fire that warmed our small bodies on those cold-nights.

Grandmother Dwa-oh, was a traditional Pueblo lady. She stood about five feet high and wore a black manta over a homemade dress, with a red, black and green sash around her middle. Her long black hair was rolled up into a chongo on the back of her head. Whenever we went to the trading post or to work in the garden, she put a towel on her head to keep the sun from shining in her eyes. However, later she went blind.

She was about 85 year old when she died. I was in nurses' training in Arizona and did not, have the privilege of caring for her in her later years. But I treasure the many things she taught me, which to this day sustain my very existence, physically, mentally, socially and definitely culturally.

As long as I can remember, I lived with Grandmother and Grandpa. My parents and siblings lived wherever the jobs were for my dad. Maybe because I was the eldest of eight children it was easier for all concerned.

In late summer and early fall we were like the animals that hibernate. We would get ready for the long, cold winter by drying fruit, cutting apples into quarters, peaches into halves and Indian melons into strips. These would turn into pies at Christmastime and on January 6 for the Laguna officers' celebration. They tasted so good after a hot, steaming bowl of pinto beans or posole.

The harvested, colored corn was separated into three piles, blue for making atole and paperbread, white for tortillas and sacred cornmeal, and the rest would be fed to animals. Some of this also was used to trade for chickens at the nearly Spanish villages, where we had many friends. Both grandparents spoke fluent Spanish as well as Keresan.

Each year at dawn on September 19th Grandpa hitched the two horses to the wagon that took us to the Laguna Feast. He and Grandmother sat up front on the seat, while I laid in the bed of the wooden vehicle watching the hills roll by and making imaginary pictures in the clouds overhead as we went bumpity bump over the dirt road.

Even before the village of Laguna was in sight, we could smell the coffee brewing from the Navajo campsites, which were scattered throughout the small mesas surrounding the pueblo. Later, they would make mutton stew, and if we found our friends from Canoncito they might invite us to eat that and fry bread.

Usually, by the time we got to the village, the Catholic Mass had already begun. But we would watch the parishioners carry the saint to an arbor built on the plaza. A Corn Dance would follow this, as well as the famous Laguna Eagle Dance.

Much trading went on between the tribes. Navajos brought silver and turquoise jewelry and rugs, Isletas came loaded with melons and green chili, while Lagunas traded the outdoor oven baked bread that they did not serve their guests at the noontime feast.

As the sun fell low in the west, it was time to return to Paguate. After Grandpa died,   Grandmother and I found other people to take us to the feast days, but we walked to the neighboring Spanish fiestas by ourselves and usually hitched a ride back with someone from Paguate.

At age twelve I left my beloved home and Grandmother for the Albuquerque Indian. School, where I lived for five years, going home in the summer for three months after that first year, then to Gallup the subsequent years; because my parents settled there.
My dad was employed by the Santa Fe Railroad at the roundhouse, and my siblings were enrolled in the public schools there. Grandmother was now living with my aunt and her family in Paguate because of impending blindness.

My first year at the boarding school was extremely traumatic. I could read and write English but did not speak the language much. I had been a straight A student at Paguate Day School, so I went from the 6th grade of that school to the 8th grade in the big school in the big city. My classmates surpassed me in the "ways of the dormitory life" and in speaking English. I cried each night under the rough khaki Army blanket on my bed in the dorm I shared with about one hundred other girls on the second floor.

This was the beginning of my transformation to another life.

—*Albuquerque Tribune*, September 17, 1998.

School and Daily Chores Form the Basis for Discipline

Once, a friend asked me where I got the discipline to walk three miles a day. I thought walking for me is not a discipline, it is a passion, an activity I do daily to appreciate the spiritual effect of a new dawning day and to retain physical strength.

True discipline I acquired through hard work and perseverance at an early age. Living with Grandmother in Paguate, I had daily chores. One was to clear the fireplace of ashes and take them to the village dump. Another was to feed the chickens. And my favorite was to fetch water from the community pump because I could play along the way with my friends.

Later, at the Albuquerque Indian School, I answered to bells for reveille, meals, class time; detail, study hour and bedtime.

Although in 1942–1947 discipline was not as strict for me as it had been for my mother in the early 1920s, I thought times were really hard. When she was a student there, she wore a uniform and marched to meals and other activities. She was also forbidden to speak her native dialect.

Many Saturdays at the school, I worked for some of my teachers in their homes, cleaning and ironing clothes. Money earned was kept in a safe in the dormitory housemother's office, and I could draw out whatever I wanted when the need arose. This was my first experience with banking.

The fund bought me snacks at the campus canteen, clothing from J.C. Penney's and Sears Roebuck in downtown Albuquerque. My friends and I had a favorite eating place when we went to town, the Coney Island at Fifth and Central for delicious hot dogs. The establishment is still there, but under a different name, and I still make an occasional visit with my twenty-one year old granddaughter.

My social gain came from intermingling with students from other tribes. Since we spoke different languages, we communicated in English. Our assigned beds in the girls' dormitory were on the first and second floors, leaving the basement for lockers and a place to socialize. We congregated there to change clothes, hear the daily campus happenings (mostly gossip) and share Pueblo bread and deer jerky from the care packages from home. A nickelodeon sat in a conspicuous place by the door, ringing tunes like "Harbor Lights," "Don't Sit Under the Apple Tree" and "Chattanooga Choo Choo."

There in the dark dungeon like room, I learned to waltz, boogie woogie and jitterbug. Eventually, I practiced these steps at the canteen if some boy asked me to dance.

Vacations from school each summer were spent in Gallup. My dad worked as a laborer in the roundhouse of the Atchison, Topeka and Santa Fe Railway. Along With my seven siblings, we lived in the boxcar Laguna community between the tracks and "The Perky" (the Rio Puerco) on the west side of town. My sister and six brothers attended public schools there. Mom kept house and I think she made a sandwich for every hobo who came from the freight trains. I lived with them at various times, but at fourteen realized I could survive on my own.

My summer jobs were mostly housekeeping and babysitting. Once, I cared for two children. My duty was to keep them clean, entertained and fed. I thought this quite easy until the day their lunch called for fried noodles and ham. I heated the skillet, threw in a dollop of lard and added the noodles. Somehow the dark brown strips of pasta dancing in the smoking pan did not look normal, so the contents went into the garbage, and the children had ham sandwiches. I should have paid more attention to my teachers in the home-ec class.

The summer of 1944, I was hired to work as a Harvey Girl and life was good!

—*Albuquerque Tribune*, November 19, 1998.

I Can Tell You, Boarding School Was Bad

I could iron seven boys' shirts in an hour when I worked in the laundry as part of my chores at the Albuquerque Indian School.

I was fourteen years old in 1944 and in the 10th grade at the boarding school, which, until about 1950, was open at 12th Street and Menaul Boulevard Northwest. I had been competing with myself for several weeks to see how rapidly I could press the government issued garments worn by some of the male students.

What I really wanted to learn while I was at school was math, world history, geography, literature and more of the English language. However, our classes were structured so that half of our time was spent doing menial tasks; farming and dairy work for the boys, kitchen and dining room chores for the girls.

Some of the half days were spent in home economics classes, the goal being to prepare us to work as domestics in someone's home. I despised this training so much that I never learned to cook well, and to this day, I would live on sandwiches if it weren't for the microwave in my kitchen and the city's numerous restaurants.

I wanted to run away from school. But I soon realized that if I did, I could end up at the Santa Fe Indian School, so many more miles away from my home in Laguna, and so I never attempted this feat.

—Albuquerque Tribune, July 2002.

Life in Boxcar Colonies in the 1940s

It was in 1885 that the railway was laid through New Mexico, which included Laguna Pueblo lands. A lump sum of money was offered to the tribe at that time for right-of-way passage by the Atchison, Topeka and Santa Fe Railway, however the tribal leaders instead requested employment on the railway for the tribal men. When the hiring began, Laguna men began leaving the villages to work in Richmond and Barstow, California, Winslow, Arizona and Gallup, New Mexico.

That is how the Laguna colonies began in those places. Families were provided railway boxcars to live in. I'm familiar with the colony in Gallup, where my dad went to work in the roundhouse in 1941, taking mom and at that time six of my siblings to reside there, while I stayed in Paguate with my grandmother.

Eventually I went to Gallup on summer vacations from the Albuquerque Indian Boarding School, and that is when I worked at El Navajo Hotel as a Harvey Girl, serving meals to the travelers.

Each boxcar dwelling, which sat next to the roundhouse and the rails, contained two rooms with six windows and a small front deck that held steps leading to two doors. A wood stove sat in the kitchen area, along with a table, bench, a cupboard for dishes and a metal icebox to hold a block of ice. The other room had as many beds as it could possibly accommodate. Community bathrooms were provided, one for men and the other for the female gender. They contained toilets, showers and bathtubs, with each household taking turns cleaning the places each day. Clotheslines and woodpiles, adjacent to the houses were evident, as was an occasional horno.

There may have been a community of twelve boxcars for as many families on the western end of that town in the 1940s. A dry riverbed separated us from the road that led to Window Rock and other places in Arizona.

As the colonies thrived in the cities they maintained a traditional tie and some mode of tribal government and were officially recognized by the Laguna Pueblo Council. They practiced tribal rituals and beliefs to a certain extent to keep them tribally connected.

Even as their parents tried to maintain the culture and traditions, the "boxcar kids" learned a way of life different from the rez. They had access to public schools, movies, stores and various activities not found in the pueblo villages, and learned the urban ways of living. They were fluent in the English language and did not learn the Keres dialect.

By 1950, my parents moved to Albuquerque where my siblings continued in public school education. My dad worked for the Bureau of Indian Affairs, and my mom as a seamstress in a tie factory on South Fourth Street.

Leaving the rez in this case provided our families the opportunities to attend schools and obtain professions of our choices.

—*Round the Roundhouse*, November 14-December 12, 2011.

I Remember My Hectic Happy Days as a Harvey Girl

In the 1870s, an Englishman by the name of Fred Harvey established, along the Atchison, Topeka and Santa Fe Railway, a chain of hotels/ dining rooms. Ranging from Chicago to San Francisco, they were called Harvey Houses.

One such hotel existed in Gallup. It was a stone structure with Navajo art decor inside. Hotel EI Navajo was founded in 1895 on the eastern edge of town between Highway 66 and the railroad tracks adjacent to Rio Puerco. The dining area opened in 1923.

I have seen the movie "Harvey Girls" starring Judy Garland, and I do not in any way relate to her character, for my life as a Harvey Girl was far less glamorous than the film portrayal.

The summer of 1944 started out with an announcement by one of Dad's relatives: "I hear they're hiring at El Navajo," to which I responded by going there and getting a job as a sandwich maker.

That whole summer a friend and I make thousands of fried egg and bologna sandwiches for the troop trains that went through Gallup. Individual sandwiches went into small, waxed paper bags, and then into cardboard boxes to go to the trains. We also made various other kinds of sandwiches for the snack shop which was part of the hotel and whose counter opened to the train track.

Some days our supervisor actually let us work in the snack shop. There, we met many interesting people who were riding the rails across America. That fall I returned to the Albuquerque Indian School with new found esteem, new clothes and money in the bank.

The next summer I advanced to a waitress in the coffee shop. My station included eight places at the horseshoe shaped black marble counter. My shift was from 6:00 a.m. to 2:30 p.m.

I really liked that job. The waitresses were required to wear white cotton blouses with long sleeves, white wraparound skirts, one size fits all and black shoes. Fingernails had to be short and clean, hair in nets above the collar, light-colored lipstick and always service with a smile.

We lived two to a room on the top floor of the hotel above the kitchen service entrance. Our house manager monitored our work performance, appearance and behavior.

The house rules and regulations at El Navajo to me were tolerable, because they were more liberal than the ones I had to live with at Albuquerque Indian School.

Gallup people who were anybody came to the Harvey House to eat. Country club ladies met for luncheons there. The Kiwanis Club had its lunch meetings in the large dining room, and the Navajo traders came in from the rez for candlelight dinners.

Also, many railroad men coming off duty ate at the counter in their work clothes of black and white striped overalls and a red bandanna neck scarf. We loved to serve those guys, because they tipped better than other people.

The favorites of most diners were the fresh hard rolls that came out of the kitchen oven several times a day and the famous Fred Harvey clam chowder, loaded with honest to goodness real clams in thick, golden, steaming hot soup.

Although there was a war on, it was an enjoyable time to be a teenager, to have a job, money, friends, fun and independence from parents.

Aside from washing my uniform on a daily basis and polishing my shoes, I read a lot, listened to the radio and went to the movies at Gallup's only two theaters to see Clark Gable, Ida Lupino and Tyrone Power. Some days some of us just "hung out" at a soda fountain to drink cherry Cokes as we fed the nickelodeon to hear "White Cliffs of Dover" or "San Antonio Rose." Although our place of employment provided our meals, we frequented some of the town cafes for hamburgers, hot dogs and fries.

A friend and I were at one of these places on August 14, 1945, VJ Day. We were sitting in a booth drinking sodas when silence was broken with screaming people on Front Street, church bells ringing, train-engine horns tooting and car horns honking. Then we saw a large mass of U.S. sailors running from the train station. They were hugging and kissing every woman they could grab. It was a frightening experience, but it was also a happy time: World War II had ended.

—*Albuquerque Tribune*, December 17, 1998.

At Seventeen I was Saying Aloha to Sea Changes in My Life

"*T*he Senior Class of the Albuquerque Indian School requests your presence at the Commencement Exercises Thursday, May the twenty ninth Nineteen hundred and forty-seven at eight o'clock p.m., Indian School Auditorium, Albuquerque, New Mexico."

So said my high school graduation announcement/invitation more than half a century ago. That night I walked to the stage in my long black robe and square topped hat with a gold tassel dangling before my eyes to receive my diploma from Veron Beggs, superintendent of schools. With shaking knees, I walked ever so carefully up several steps in my Cuban-heeled black patent-leather pumps, hoping that I would not trip and fall.

Aside from being nervous, I was full of joy at having completed a goal, and how I could move onto another. At age seventeen, I was looking toward being a nurse. Having completed all graduation requirements of high school academics by December 1946, I had chosen to remain with the class to engage in the social functions of the last months that we would be together, continuing to attend classes, of course, mostly of elective subjects.

The senior trip to Carlsbad Caverns a month before we left school was one of the highlights of our spring activities. We went in a bus to White's City and toured the caverns the next day. Eating peanut-butter sandwiches by the roadside in San Antonio, New Mexico, was our dinner before the return to school on that trip. The money for the excursion was raised through a benefit carnival in the school gym.

We involved our teachers in the project. They read palms as gypsies, donated pastry for the cakewalk, and gave us their unwanted trinkets for fishpond prizes and a white elephant sale.

Some of us from the class volunteered to put on a theater play called the "Bobby Sox Brigade," about a lively teenage girl and her sister, who was a nerd. I was the nerd sister. The cast also included the girls' mother, a house-maid, the wild teen's boyfriend and a milkman. The rehearsals extended to drinking R.C. Colas and dancing at the canteen after practice sessions,

There I became better acquainted with the milkman actor, who later took me to the senior banquet, the prom and the memorable last senior dance, where he presented me with a sweet smelling gardenia corsage. He was a tall, lean fellow with a frequent friendly smile that added to his glowing personality. His intellect and sense of humor won him the president's post of both the senior class and the Student Council.

Time raced that spring in 1947. I participated in the Glee Club, Girl Scouts, the soccer team and worked on the school's yearbook, called *The Sandpainter*, I even wrote (with another girl) our senior class song to the tune of *Aloha Oe*.

Today, it is hard to imagine that so many years before; one pathetic little twelve year old girl had cried in the big yellow school bus that brought her to this city, now her home. Away from the freedom of running about the Paguate mesas to catch butterflies and gather wild celery and onions. Leaving behind the revered ceremonial dances, with Keres the only language she knew and the delicate memories of Grandmother, who had been her caretaker and mentor in her early years.

In five years, the school and the Bureau of Indian Affairs had almost successfully Americanized me. It had taught me the English language and the ways of white America as it tried to strip me of my own language, my heritage, my culture and my dress.

Today, however, I am better for it. I can cope and survive in both worlds, taking the best from each culture as I want or need them.

In 1998, the Albuquerque Indian School no longer exists. In its place is a dry deserted vacant lot at Twelfth and Menaul. There, eventually, will stand an upper-class hotel with 250 suites, an elegant dining room, a performing arts theater, retail shops and a first-rate pueblo museum.

—*Albuquerque Tribune*, January 28 1999.

My graduation from the Albuquerque Indian School.

Teaching's in the Blood, But I Set My Cap on Nursing

*T*he three of them were elementary school teachers, mom and two of her sisters.

Aunt Kate, for whom I am named, taught on the Navajo Reservation until age thirty; when she died there of tuberculosis. Mom taught until there were too many of us children at home to be cared for. Aunt Rachel stayed with the profession well, into her 50s and taught me in several classes at Paguate Day School.

During my last year at Albuquerque Indian School, my parents often wrote in letters to me, "Nursing is hard; don't you think you should go into teaching?" Meaning: "Can you stand the physical endurance and the mental stability that nursing requires?"

My desire to become a nurse came when I was seven years old. I'd had a tonsillectomy at the Indian Hospital. which in 1936 was located at Twelfth Street Northwest in Albuquerque near Interstate-40 and the nurses who cared for me impressed me with their kindness and generosity. Also, they looked beautiful in their white dresses and caps. I wanted to be like them, one day.

In the fall of 1947, I entered the Sage Memorial Hospital School of Nursing. I carried to the hospital administrator a check for $350 for my first year's tuition. This paid for books, instruction, room and board, lab fees, six white uniforms and, a navy blue woolen nurse's cape.

The hospital, at Ganado, Arizona, was situated on one of the largest Presbyterian missions in the United States. The community was made up of two acres on the Navajo Reservation, 56 miles northwest of Gallup. With 60 buildings on campus, the mission had its own farm, dairy, laundry and powerhouse.

The primary purpose of the Ganado Mission High School was to train native peoples in spiritual, educational, economic and physical growth. The hospital trained nurses in a three-year diploma program.

The natural-stone-built Sage Memorial Hospital was erected in 1929 and took its name from the Olivia Sage Memorial Fund. Accredited by the

Joint Commission on Hospital Accreditation, the facility contained 60 beds and 12 bassinets, and had an active outpatient department. It was a well-equipped, first class hospital with a surgical suite, delivery room, laboratory, diet kitchen, pharmacy and X-ray department. Emergency care, surgery and obstetrical services were readily available.

Thirteen of us girls started as "probationers," that's what they called the beginning students. We came from five states. As the school required, we represented people of minority descent; Spanish, Mexican, Eskimo and six American Indian tribes.

In our house, the Florence Nightingale Lodge, we lived two to a room, with two beds, two chairs, a table; a dresser and a small closet. Our eighty year old missionary housemother made sure we were always in bed by ten each night. Once a month she collected us into the living room for cookies and punch. Otherwise, she was available 24 hours a day for us to cry on her shoulder or to share in our joys.

Entertainment there was rare. We could take an occasional dip in the pool or attend a Saturday night movie, both on the campus, with the high school students and employees.

Our schedule was: at 5:30 a.m., wash and get correctly dressed in white uniforms, hose and shoes; 6:15 a.m., devotions; 6:30 a.m., wash patients for breakfast; 7:30 a.m., breakfast in the campus dining room; 8:30 a.m., in the classroom until lunch time; then back to class until 4:30 p.m., We learned nursing arts, which included giving direct patient care, taking blood pressures and temperatures. We also learned the history of nursing and medicine, sociology, psychology, anatomy and physiology.

Unknown to us at the time, as we were studying in our own little niche and marveling at Madame Marie Curie's discovery of radium in the early 1900s, the world powers in 1948 were in the midst of developing the herculean hydrogen bomb.

At the end of six months, one of our classmates left out of loneliness, so there were twelve of us at the capping ceremony in early March.

We had passed numerous tests, both in the classrooms and on the patient care we gave.

We stood side by side that one glorious evening in the chapel, each holding a ceramic Florence Nightingale lamp with a tiny candle that illuminated our happy faces. We were no longer "probies." We were student nurses and had a cap to prove it.

—*Albuquerque Tribune*, February18, 1999.

With my fellow nursing students.

The Busy Days and On-call Nights of Nursing

I stood in the tiny utility room of Capital Hospital in Beijing, China, on March 17, 1983, and stared at the aluminum pan boiling syringes and hypodermic needles over an electric hotplate.

Outdoors, the gusty, cold wind blew fine white dust from Mongolia, making the city almost invisible. Inside, steaming vapors from the utensils brought the atmosphere to near coziness.

The process on the stove immediately reminded me of the times I prepared morphine and codeine for injections when I was a student nurse in 1949. Needles and syringes were sterilized by boiling them in water. Then they were removed and placed in a sterile container.

To prepare for a shot, a spoon of water was boiled over a Bunsen burner, a tiny gas burner that produced a hot, blue flame. When that water cooled down, twelve units were drawn up in a glass syringe, allowing the rest to be wasted. Then the narcotic pill was dissolved in the spoon by water in the syringe.

Only after careful manipulation, preparation and calculation was the medication given to the ailing patient

Pharmacology, the science dealing with the effect of drugs on living organisms, was one of our courses of study as junior nursing students.

Medicines during that era did not come in pre-packaged units as they do today, so it was up to the nurse to calculate and prepare much of this for administration. Therefore, we had to have a keen knowledge of math and chemistry, as well as the metric and apothecary systems.

Also, in those days drugs were not as numerous as they are now. A special yellow page in my 1949 Textbook of Pharmacology for Nurses reads: "Penicillin, a new antibiotic agent derived from a mold, is presumed to be somewhat similar to that of sulfonamides, that is, its primary effect is to prevent multiplication of bacteria." The drug supplied in dry form was dissolved in sterile physiologic saline solution and given intramuscularly every four hours.

As second-year students, we now wore a small, black-velvet stripe on the right corner of our caps, and with this mark of prestige came many new responsibilities.

One major subject that challenged most of us was obstetrics, caring for women in labor, delivery and postpartum. We had by now completed medical and surgical nursing and were into a more complex mode.

To graduate, we were required to "scrub" for a certain number of deliveries. Some of these calls to assist in the delivery room came at night, which meant getting out of bed and into full uniform and racing to the hospital. We set up basins of water, a sterile field of forceps, scissors, sutures, needles, syringes and the medicines pitocin, which contracts the uterus, and ergotrate, to prevent postpartum bleeding. Cans of ether and masks had to be available for possible anesthesia.

Split shifts on duty were necessary to accommodate our classes during the day, when we learned the theories of procedures we were doing and of ones yet to come.

What little social life we had during nine months of that year became practically nil now. We were attending Presbyterian church services on Sunday mornings and Thursday evening prayer meetings if we were not on duty.

Just as life was hard at this time, it was also extremely interesting to learn about the human body and its functions in normal and abnormal states.

Classes ceased for three months in summer, when we took turns going home for three weeks at a time. Those left at school provided nursing services to the hospital.'

Days off were treasured times. With High School students gone, we had greater access to the swimming pool, park and tennis courts. Some days our 80-year-old house mother took us hiking to Ganado Hills, the lake and Hubbell's Trading Post several miles away from the campus

My parents were in Chicago in June 1949 with my three youngest brothers and sister performing Laguna Pueblo dances at the Atchison, Topeka and Santa Fe Railway Fair when my vacation was due.

I did not join them there, but instead went to Laguna to be with Aunt Rachel and her family and with Grandmother. It was the last time I would see my beloved Dwa-oh my grandmother, for she died the next spring.

—*Albuquerque Tribune*, March 3, 1999.

Our living quarters at Ganado.

In 1950, We Truly Became Professionals

"Oh, my goodness, how do they sterilize those things?" I asked of the clear plastic intravenous tubing I saw for the first time in 1950, knowing only how the rubber tubing worked for the IV infusions. "They don't resterilize them, they throw them away," my classmate replied. I stood in awe, looking at this wonderful object that, twenty-five years later, I would be teaching about as Nursing Specialist in Intravenous Therapy.

The second black stripe on the right corner of our caps signified that we were seniors in August 1949, and that we had in fact become the backbone of the nursing staff at Sage Memorial Hospital. Professional nursing and recordkeeping courses were intensified during this time. Our other subjects were public health nursing, psychiatry, diet, postmortem care and giving intravenous drugs and solutions.

Scrubbing for surgical cases in the operating room was an exciting way to learn more about anatomy and physiology, by looking inside a person and seeing the functions and dysfunctions of a human body. We had a few favorite surgeons to work with, the kind, cool ones who did not throw instruments in anger. Our surgical supervisor stood immediately behind us in the operating room, monitoring our every move so she could grade our performance. She also taught us how to clean, package and sterilize surgical and obstetrical instruments in an autoclave, a steam sterilizing unit.

Rotation to outpatient/emergency department was a provocative experience. I watched Navajo elders die from pneumonia and tuberculosis right in the clinic. Babies and small children brought in with sunken eyes, high fever and unconsciousness from typhoid fever did survive a hypodermaclysis (fluids given with needles under skin) in our attempts to rehydrate them. But they died soon after admission to the isolation unit. It was a time I questioned God and the U.S. Indian Health Service.

Special duty, caring for one patient after surgery or one in critical condition, was part of our training before intensive and coronary care units came on the scene. Preventing bed sores, inserting tubes into various body orifices, starting intravenous solutions, calculating intake and output and just making the patient as comfortable as possible prepared us to go out into the world as well trained, qualified bedside nurses.

Night duty, taking complete charge of a floor on the 11 p.m. to 7 a.m. shift gave us practice in checking doctor's orders, patients' charts, lab and X-ray work to be done in the morning. We made the work schedule for other nurses to follow; this was called nursing management.

During our last year, a girl transferred from Tucson to join us, and we were thirteen again. By May 1950, we were making plans for graduation in August. The diploma would allow us to work as graduate nurses, but we would still have to take Arizona State Board exams in Phoenix that fall to qualify as registered nurses if we passed the two day set of test questions.

I was to return to Albuquerque, get a job at Presbyterian Hospital and help care for grandmother, who was now eighty-five and blind. But this was not to be. Almost as soon as my plans were being formulated, the painful news of her death was relayed to me by Mom in writing. My chance to grieve for her did not come until the next spring, when I returned to the home where she had given me loving care. Today, I still feel her spirit beside me.

In June of 1950, North Korea invaded South Korea and America sent troops there, Stunned at the news, my friend Josie and I talked about joining the Army Nurse Corps.

So for the last time, on August 23, 1950, at 8 p.m., my classmates and I stood together in Ganado Mission's chapel, this time dressed in long-sleeved uniforms, a small shield shaped school pin on the left chest and a cap with a full black stripe. Each carrying a candle lit Florence Nightingale ceramic lamp, we recited:

"I solemnly pledge myself before God and in the presence of this assembly to pass my life in purity and to practice my profession faithfully. I will abstain from whatever is deleterious and mischievous and will not take or knowingly administer any harmful drug. I will do all in my power to maintain and elevate the standard of my profession and will hold in confidence all personal matters committed to my keeping and all family affairs coming to my knowledge in the practice of my calling. With loyalty will I endeavor to aid the physician in his work and devote myself to the welfare of those committed to my care."

May 6 is Nurses Day, and in their honor this article is dedicated.

—*Albuquerque Tribune,* April 15, 1999.

A play day for the nurses in Gallup.

Path to Nursing Led Away from Korea, Toward Duke City

I did not go to the war in Korea in 1950. By the time I received word that I had become a registered nurse, Dad and a male friend had convinced me that I should not be there.

Also, my friend Josie was writing me disparaging letters from a M.A.S.H. unit somewhere in South Korea: "Don't join the Army, we're up to our knees in mud, we can only have showers three times a week, it's awful here; stay where you are."

I stayed at Fort Defiance Medical Center for four months, but the longing to return to Albuquerque became overwhelming, so I left the Navajo "rez" for good.

In early 1951, I found myself applying for nursing jobs along East Central Avenue. Presbyterian Hospital and the Atchison, Topeka and Santa Fe Railway Hospital, now Memorial Hospital. Each took my application and promised to call me when positions became available. I walked farther west to the Women's and Children's Hospital, where I was hired.

The "W&C" at High Street and Central had once been a home. The two-story, white building had offices, a kitchen and a dining room on the first floor. Upstairs were a small operating room, delivery room, four bassinets in the newborn nursery, a six-bed ward and several private rooms. The nursing station at the top of the stairs had a window that looked down at busy Route 66 traffic and a hamburger joint across the street.

The nursing experience I received there was invaluable, and I truly enjoyed working with the patients. Doctors, nurses, maids, janitors and kitchen workers were like a family.

That fall I was married. The next year I moved to Barstow, California, a Godforsaken little town in the Mojave Desert, to be a housewife for two years—a definite maladjustment on my part.

Upon my return to Albuquerque, I reapplied at the Presbyterian Hospital and took the position of head nurse on their newly established, sixty-four bed Tubercular Navajo Children's Unit in the two-story Minister's

Building, the main hospital before Presbyterian grew, across the street from Maytag.

I supervised several nurses and aides and directed the nursing care and daily activities of children ages six months to twelve years. Many of the children who were not bedridden had a teacher. Streptomycin, INH and vitamins were their only medications, rest and nutrition being the other aspect of their therapy.

In a few years tuberculosis was eradicated on the Navajo reservation, and our hospital census declined. The few remaining children were returned to hospitals near their homes, and our contract with the federal government ended. I transferred as staff nurse to the main part of the hospital. This meant learning about newer equipment, medications and some procedures. It also meant meeting many new people, doctors, nurses, technicians and other hospital workers.

At this time, too, I was making changes in my personal life. My marriage ended, causing me to become a single parent at age twenty-nine, with custody of children who were ages three, six and seven. I realized then that I would have to reevaluate my life plans and refocus on various other aspects of survival. With this, I set out on a new beginning. I had the promise of a job, dreams of fulfilling several goals and a better life for the kids and me.

I was to work at Presbyterian for twenty-nine years in pediatrics, newborn nursery, medical/surgical units and an occasional stint in the emergency room. Advancing from a staff nurse to head nurse to nurse-educator, my career was indeed on an upward swing.

Each phase was an exciting period. As staff nurse, I loved giving treatments and medicines; they took me to the patient's bedside. As head nurse I worked with doctors, made the nurses time schedules and assignments. I had to know all forty patients on my floor, each of their names, ages, diagnoses and lab and X-ray results. I traveled to all eleven Presbyterian managed hospitals in the state when I became an educator with a specialty in intravenous therapy.

Teaching nurses was the most rewarding part of my occupation. It took me to many places around the world.

—*Albuquerque Tribune,* May 20, 1999

I have become a professional nurse.

The Laguna Colony of Albuquerque

resh carnations and tiny white flowers in glass vases decorated the white tables at Laguna Colony's annual Christmas party on December 5th at the Albuquerque Indian Center. Twinkling colored lights and evergreens graced the serving table alongside steaming pots of red and green chili stews, Pueblo bread, ham, turkey, vegetables and desserts. With carols playing in the background, sixty-five Colony members, aged from a few weeks to ninety years, had come for the "gathering-of-the-clans" at the festive affair.

In the early 1950s, a small group of Laguna tribal members living in Albuquerque carne together and established this unique urban Indian organization called The Laguna Colony of Albuquerque. Today approximately 300 tribal members are property-owning, tax-paying citizens of this city. Meeting once a month at St. Andrews Presbyterian Church, they stay in contact with current policies and events at Laguna Pueblo. "A Colony member is a recognized member of Laguna Pueblo residing in the Albuquerque Metropolitan area and other Laguna Pueblo members who on a voluntary basis desire to be Colony members. A non-Laguna spouse and/or children of Colony members may be recognized as associate members," the bylaws state.

Colony officer elections take place the first Tuesday in December. The first order of each agenda is the reading of Colony minutes, then the Laguna Pueblo assembly recordings.

Reports are made by committee chairs of finance, social, state fair concession, education and Laguna cultural teachings. These groups oversee the Colony's concession at the New Mexico State Fair's Indian Village as well as its social functions (parties and picnics), Laguna language (Keres) teaching and educational scholarship awards.

By December 21st Laguna Colony members have cast their votes by absentee ballot or by going to the Pueblo to elect their tribal Governor, Lieutenant Governor, Secretary, Treasurer, Interpreter and Staff Officer. On December 31st some of these urban Lagunas join the village residents in the installation of new officers. On stage at the community house outgoing officers have placed on a table the revered Lincoln canes, given to the tribe by President Abraham Lincoln as a sign of authority. After the blessing of the canes by a Franciscan Friar and a tribal religious leader, they are given to the new officers. Both English and Keresean languages are used at this inspiring ceremony.

Many Laguna Colony members leave Albuquerque each January 6th to "go home" for an evening celebration of the newly elected officers. Buffalo, deer, eagle and other dances are performed throughout six of the eight Laguna villages with the Colony members taking part in various aspects of the festivity. At midnight families gather for feasting on red chili posole, horno baked bread and Indian fruit pies. The New Year has officially begun for the Laguna people.

—Albuquerque Tribune, May 20, 1999

Tales My Grandmother Told Me and Being Laguna

Some of the stories that follow were told to me by my grandmother when I was a little girl growing up at Laguna Pueblo. I have also included my observations of pueblo life and experiences. The images of ancient petroglyphs that accompany these stories all from Central New Mexico found in the vicinity of Laguna. They were made by my ancestors who probably told the same stories and had similar experiences.

The Hunt for Wild Celery

"*D*wa-oh, Granddaughter, pick only the ones without flowers and seeds," she said of the wild celery. "When plants get mature enough to bloom, they are no longer tender and we must leave the seeds for next year's crop," she explained. I walked about five paces ahead of her, looking downward for the objects of our hunt. Grandmother knew many things; she taught me how to find the celery and wild onions, also how to pick wild tea and make the plants into bundles; she even showed me how to make red chili rabbit stew. Each April, when I was a small child at Laguna Pueblo, she and I walked beyond the edge of our village to the hills to gather the delectable morsels.

From under the straggly cedar tree branches the frozen snow had melted, leaving in its place small sand dunes brought on by the vigorous gusts of the early spring winds. In the remote quietness, surrounded by clear fresh air with a mild arid breeze, we walked past the cactus plants and a few Indian paintbrushes not yet in bloom. When the celery came into view, the flour sack was unrolled and opened up for our stash. After a wet season the plants, which usually have one-to two-inch leaves, were larger, greener and glossier. They seemed to hug the soil but were easy to pick. We decided to add some wild onions. These were a real challenge! With only one tiny stem barely visible above the ground, we had to dig five or six inches for the fur-covered bulb as tiny as an infants little finger.

The pungent vegetables, after being washed under running water, were ready to be eaten with a pinch of salt and outdoor-oven-baked bread or a tortilla.

The rest would be dried and packed for later use. They would flavor the boiled pinto beans and the stews made with corn and meat. As the sun rose high toward the west in the bright blue cloudless sky, we made our way back home, but not before we thanked the Spirit of Mother Earth for our bountiful gathering as did our ancestors thousands of years ago.

—*Pueblo Horizons*, Spring 1996.

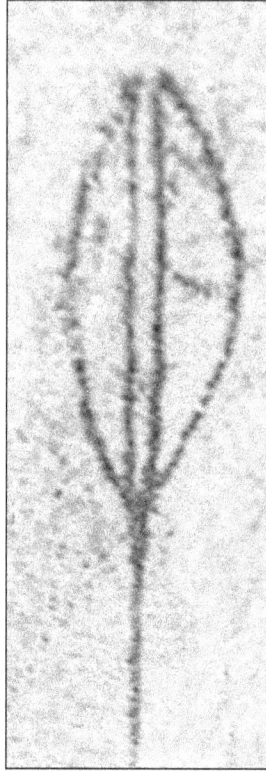

Wild celery.

The Deer Hunter

"On this mountain we hear you sing in the kind, gentle wind that blows through the pine trees. We feel your breath in the early morning dew. O Great Spirit, keeper of the eagle and the deer, we ask for courage and strength for this day. I, Go-Te-May, am ready to be a deer-hunter," Jeremy bragged to his father and grandfather, as the three stepped out of the tent into the cold November dawn on Mount Taylor. The eight-year-old Pueblo Indian youth was about to venture into the forest with the two men for the hunt, the experience that would become a great part of his life.

The boy had been preparing for this time since the day Grandfather told him a "long ago" story. They had been working in the cornfield below the village where they lived, when a sudden rainstorm erupted and they had to run into a small adobe house to stay dry. Grandfather had built this shelter many years before Jeremy was born; there he usually ate his lunches of dried deer meat and tortillas before returning to his chores in the fields. As the large noisy slap, slap of the raindrops turned into soft quiet sprinkles of water, the whole earth seemed new again: the corn stalks were greener, the melon vines were more visible and the scent of the wet ground made Jeremy want to taste it. Now the sunlight had come through and there was a glistening mist with a brilliant multicolored rainbow. "Na-Na Grandson, whenever it rains like this, the Old Ones say that a baby deer is born, Grandfather informed Jeremy. "You must always remember that the deer is very important to our people; it gives us food and its hide we use for moccasins. We respect this great animal by having a ceremonial dinner with our family and clan members, and a dance is held in its honor."

So impressed was Jeremy with this story that he could hardly wait to grow big enough to deer hunt. Now the day had finally arrived. The cool autumn breeze played on his little brown ears and cheeks, while each footstep of his heavy boots made a crunch sound on the dry pine needles and fallen branches. Deep in the wilderness Grandfather stood in reverence to sprinkle the sacred cornmeal in the four directions, asking the ShiWa-Na, the Great

Spirit for the hunt, and also making an apology to the deer for the sacrificial slaying that would take place. This, Jeremy learned, was the way of the Pueblo People.

"Shhhhhh," Jeremy's father whispered softly, as he turned to the young boy and his grandfather. "I think I see something out there," the experienced deer-hunter continued. Jeremy's father walked several paces ahead of the other two, with his gun over his left shoulder. There before them through the Hay-ya-Shh, a small fog above a pond, were four deer drinking water: two bucks, a doe and a fawn. Jeremy's eyes grew round as did his mouth; it was such a phenomenal sight to him that he thought his heart would burst. Then the animals' ears perked up; they sniffed and stared before springing away in huge graceful leaps.

Jeremy did not see, nor did he hear, his father cock the gun. It was only when he felt the loud boom, which made him jump, that he saw the buck fall to the ground. The boy was not sure if it was all right to cry. The feeling of life going out of the lovely animal made him sad, but he was also overcome by the exciting, wonderful experience of "catching a deer." His tear filled eyes seemed to release both emotions. Once again Grandfather reached into the bright-colored, bead-decorated buckskin pouch, with it strap over his left shoulder. He gave a handful of sacred cornmeal to each hunter—yes, even to Jeremy, who was now a hunter. "Da-Wa-Eh," they prayed, thankful for the deer that would accompany them back to the village. On the very mountain Go-Te that Jeremy was named for stood the young hunter, who now embraced one aspect of his Pueblo Indian life. Releasing the cornmeal on the deer's head, Jeremy with a glad heart murmured, "Welcome, let us take you to your place of honor in our home."

—*Pueblo Horizons*, Fall 1996.

Killing a deer.

The Rabbit Hunt

Here on the mesa, I hear your voice
in the gentle breeze.
Your breath I feel
in the warm sunshine.
Give me strength to walk these hills.
Da-Wa-Eh

Everything in the air seemed pure and dry that warm spring day in 1940. I was eleven years old and was allowed by Grandmother to join her in the rabbit hunt for the first time. Brimming with joy and excitement, I walked eagerly with several dozen men and women eastward out of the small village of Paguate, one of the Laguna Pueblo communities.

In the brilliant sunlight, birds flew out of the cedar trees which bore tart tasting blue berries, lizards moved at great speed to hide under flat rocks, and nearby a mourning dove called. We slid down shallow arroyos lined with shining clean sand and were careful not to brush up against the yuccas that were just beginning to bloom. Wild celery and onions had just begun to appear so they would hot be ready for harvesting for another month.

The men walked ahead tracking footprints and beating the bushes with knot-headed clubs. If one happened to kill a rabbit, the women ran to get the prize.

Starting in the morning and going some distance from the village, the whole community participated in the hunt. It lasted until late in the afternoon, away from the vegetable gardens and melon patches.

The communal rabbit hunt dates back to the Basketmaker era of the Pueblo ancestors. A century ago, the Pueblo Indians still hunted for prairie dogs and rabbits for sustenance. I remember sixty years ago that my grandfather set out traps in the corn fields for them.

A real delicacy, the rabbit was skinned, gutted, cut up and made into red chili stew. It was eaten with freshly made flour tortillas or bread made in the homo, the dome-shaped outdoor oven. Savory tasting orange-colored tea, brewed on top of Grandmother's wood stove, was our beverage

At noontime we stopped for rest and for a bite to eat. Grandmother and I found a tiny bit of shade next to some sagebrush, and she opened up the flour sack for the jar of water, two corn tortillas and a hunk of goat cheese, which we relished. The women who had gotten rabbits returned home at this time.

Suddenly, a yell came from one of the men. I jumped up from the ground and ran as fast as my short, thin legs could carry me, leaving behind Grandmother and the other women. Almost out of breath, I collected the hare that was almost too heavy for me to carry. "Da-Wa-Eh (Thank you)," I told the hunter, then waited for Grandmother to help me take it home.

As in every Pueblo event that is of a religious nature, I thanked the Great Spirit for this bounty, then in the kitchen prepared a basket of food for the hunter to take to his house. This was to wish him well on all his future hunts.

—*Pueblo Horizons*, Summer 1998.

The rabbit.

The Tale of Two Sashes

"We the people of Lithuania honor you today. Take this to reminder of the work you have done for us and our deep gratitude for your effort," Vida Balseine, Director of Nurses, said to me as she placed the "best worker" bronze medal award in my right hand and a single red rose-on-a-stem in my left. "And wear it with pride," she added adorning me with a red, green and tan colored woven Lithuanian ceremonial sash over my right shoulder, tying it at the left waist.

Moved to tears of elation, sadness and some relief, I tried to contain my heartfelt emotions in the auditorium of Vilnius University Hospital as one hundred nurses and doctors stood to applaud. It was Friday, October 16, 1992, my last day at the Health Institute where for one week I had observed, listened and given technical advice in the science of Intravenous Therapy, my nursing specialty. In that time I had grown fond of the people I was in contact with. People-to-People International had invited me to participate in this Baltic nation's request for advice in management, training and implementation in this field of nursing. So here I was half way around the world from my homeland.

On the plane bound for St. Petersburg, formerly known as Leningrad, I took the sash out of the flight bag for my Ambassador associates to admire. Upon its return to its special place in the bag, I was reminded of another place and another time. Through the skies and clouds of Russia I thought of that one day in Paguate, Laguna Pueblo.

I was seven years old, and it was St. Elizabeth Feast Day. Grandmother was dressing me for my first Harvest dance on September 25, 1936. She put the homemade flowered-print cotton dress on me, carefully smoothing out all the wrinkles, then the black manta trimmed with red and green yarn. Next came the Pueblo ceremonial sash woven in striking colors of red, green and black. This she wrapped many times around my tiny waist, and while doing this she told me: "Your grandfather made many of these before he died. They were given to relatives, and this may be the last one left in this house, so take

58

good care of it, wear it with pride and joy for it is part of the traditional dress of our people."

The colorful back apron with a wide purple ribbon border and a string of coral bead necklace completed the dress. Since I did not have moccasins to wear on my feet, I wore the only shoes I had, U.S. government-issued black high-top shoes over brown cotton stockings.

Grandmother combed and braided my long black hair into two plaits, rubbed Vaseline ointment on my face, and I was ready to go dance. The screen door slammed behind me as I skipped into the brilliant morning sunshine on my way to the kiva to have my hands painted with the white clay of Mother Earth.

Suddenly, the changing sound of Aeroflot's engine returned me to the present. We were about to land and I could see the canals and tall buildings of St. Petersburg. Today, in my home the Lithuanian and Pueblo sashes hang side by side on a wall, signifying two momentous days in my life.

—*Pueblo Horizons*, Spring 1999.

An ancient sash.

The Sacred Rocks

"*D*o you think Kokopelli played his flute here?" Ten-year-old Jake asked his mother. "He may have, he seemed to be everywhere." The tall, slender, young Pueblo woman replied, as a sudden gust of wind blew her long raven-black hair across her face. Under cobalt blue skies, the two were looking at the petroglyphs on the West Mesa of Albuquerque. An occasional hawk circled above their heads on this clear warm day in April, while the coo of a mourning dove was heard from a distant cedar tree. Lizards appeared and flippantly made their way around the volcanic rocks there.

"I wish I could have watched the Indians draw and carve these stars and birds on the rocks." Jake further commented. "If Jon and I were living then, I bet we could have done that too." Speaking of his fourteen year-old cousin who was an up and coming young Oklahoma artist.

"My teacher said that a long time ago, the Native Americans lived in pit houses along the Rio Grande. They were houses that were partially underground. Wow!" He exclaimed, "the kids had a swimming pool in their front yard and could swim any time they wanted to. They didn't have to sit in some boring classroom to learn math, English, and history. It must have been fun to be a kid then." The boy surmised.

"No Jake," his mother interrupted, "the kids didn't have to sit in a classroom, this whole mesa and beyond was their school." She explained that the children had to learn how to hunt for food in order to survive. They learned the language of their people, about Sipapu, where the people came from and tribal traditions.

They danced as soon as they could walk and sang as soon as they could talk. The kachina petroglyphs are evidence that the people were religious people then, as they are even today. When one attends a ceremonial dance, the rhythmic drumbeat and the sacred songs of the Pueblo people pertain to the many beautiful petroglyphs etched on the rocks. A testimony to the longevity of the people.

Listen and you will hear them sing of the plants, of the water, of the animals, of the mountains. The Pueblo people embrace this land in a way other people cannot understand.

—*Laguna Colony Info Page*, March 20 1998.

Kokopelli playing his flute.

A Pueblo Harvest

Corn, gleaming in the sun
Yellow, red, purple, and blue.
Corn, a gift to the Hano,
The Pueblo People.

*T*he warm Indian Summer day started out as a cool, crisp morning, birds chirping wildly in the huge apple-tree growing next to the window of the room where I slept as a five-year-old child.

Grandmother awakened me to remind me that today we were to husk the dry corn that lay in a pile on the south side of our adobe house. The colorful grain had been brought from the fields several days before by Grandfather, using a wagon hitched to two horses.

It was fall in Paguate, a Laguna Pueblo community located about ten miles north of the mother village. The apricots, peaches, plums and apples had been dried, placed in flour sacks, and now hung over a wooden rack in the semi dark storage room adjacent to the U-shaped main house. Jars of purple grape jelly and red tomatoes decorated the wooden shelves that sat in the small ray of sunlight beaming through one tiny window. In the dead of winter the dried fruit would be steamed and made into pies, and the jelly would be spread on a warm tortilla or fry-bread for a delicious dessert. Tomatoes cooked with macaroni would be sooo good.

"Dwa-oh, granddaughter, save the large husks for wrapping tamales," Grandmother instructed me, as she did every year at this time. "The blue corn will go in this tub," she gestured with a nod of her head to the left, and, waving her right hand outward, she continued, "The white ones go here, and the rest will go back in the wagon to go to the barn for the animals."

Each late September our corn crop was carefully preserved for winter use. Blue com kernels ground on a metate with a mano would provide blue cornmeal to be made into atole (com mush), a warm satisfying cereal on a cold winter morning. In the evening, atole in beverage form served as a drink to be sipped as we sat in front of the corner fireplace crackling with burning pinion wood, while Grandfather told us children "long ago" stories.

Blue cornmeal was also used to make paper-bread. The thin batter, spread by hand on a fire-heated flat rock, blistered into sheets of blue bread. When folded, it could be eaten with red chili mutton stew or pinto beans.

White cornmeal tortillas were cooked on top of the wood stove and looked like huge pancakes. Many times they served as bread. For tamales, red chili meat sauce was covered by thick white cornmeal. The mixture was then enveloped in the precious corn husks we had saved earlier. A portion of the white cornmeal would be retained for use as a blessing at prayer times.

Corn grinding is a ceremony in itself. Grandmother had a special room with three sets of metates and manos where she and two other women got down on their knees to grind corn and wheat. Grandfather sat to one side and sang songs that kept their movements in rhythm. These songs expressed the thankful spirit of the harvest, grateful for all that sustains the Hano, the Pueblo People.

—*Pueblo Horizons*, Fall 1997.

Corn.

A Winter Celebration at Laguna Pueblo

*T*he magical quiet time of the Winter Solstice was evident in Paguate, a community that is part of Laguna Pueblo and lies ten miles north of the mother village. It nestles in a valley surrounded by mesas and small rolling hills. On that early afternoon on Christmas Day 1995, Mount Taylor to the west beamed on me as its cover of snow brought to reality that it was the winter season.

Gone were the usual noisy sounds of a Pueblo feast day celebration when people gather to witness dances in the plaza, gone also were the hamburger stands, the arts and crafts tables, and the bustling public. It was still a celebration but one of peace and tranquility. The people sat on chairs and benches wrapped in colorful wool Pendleton blankets as they watched the deer and buffalo dances. Even the drumming and the singing of the men's chorus seemed muted and gave a sense of solemnity. In the clean crisp air the delicious aroma of posole cooking was present, as was the scent of the burning pinion wood from the stoves that were keeping warm the unique New Mexico dish. The visual effect of the adobe homes in the winter sun was an artist's dream.

Forty men, of all ages even down to only six years, were taking part in the deer dance. Each was wearing a headdress of evergreens with antlers sticking out on the crown, while more greens graced the waist and the upper arm of each dancer. An embroidered kilt was secured by a red, green, and black Pueblo sash. The bells below the dancer's knees made tinkling sounds as they stepped up and down in rust colored buckskin moccasins. The white sticks they carried in each hand as deer's forelegs gave a definite image of the beautiful animal that the men and boys were portraying. The two buffalo dancers were dressed in a similar fashion except for headgear made of goat skins. These pelts were dyed a dark color, with two horns protruding out of each to portray a buffalo's head. A fan of feathers adorned each headdress, and these decorations fluttered in the ever so slight northerly wind or when the "buffaloes" moved to this dance of speed and precision. Each dancer's right hand held a gourd rattle which, when shaken, made the noise of precious falling rain, while the left hand gestured with a bow and arrow. A girl dancer, elaborately dressed in traditional black manta with a woven white Hopi shawl covering her shoulders, kept in motion to every crescendo of the drum beat. Her feet seemed never to touch the ground as she waved hand-held wood-carved flowers in prayer.

"Goo-wa-ze" I greeted my relatives, noting how my Keresan dialect returns each time I come back to my ancestral home. This language has always been very meaningful and powerful to me so that, when anyone speaks in Keres to me, I know the words are coming from the heart. At my cousin's house, my face and hands no longer felt old. I could not decide whether the warmth came from eating the red chili posole or from the glowing flames in the corner fireplace. Also, it may have been from the sheer excitement of being home again, for Paguate is where I learned the rich Pueblo way of life and where my soul is.

—*Pueblo Horizons*, Winter 1996.

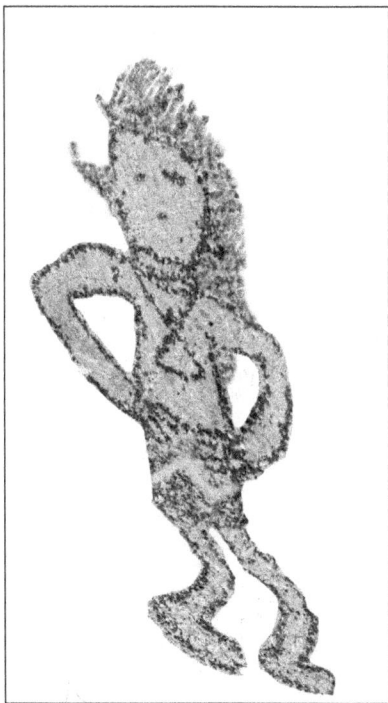

The buffalo dancer.

Seama Feast

*T*hree colorful butterflies dance alongside the mighty buffalo as Corn dancers move briskly to song and a rhythmic drumbeat.

White thunderheads above the plaza look down in solemn prayer.

July 26th this year started out mostly sunny but with some clouds in the sky. The small Laguna village of Seama was having its annual feast day. Readily seen from Interstate 40 just before you reach Cubero and San Fidel, it is next to the Acoma reservation. Nestled in the midst of three hills, it has its own unique personality with its three little suburbs of Harrisburg, New York and Philadelphia (so named by the residents who returned from Carlisle Indian School in Pennsylvania in the late 1800s). My father was from Philadelphia, so I have numerous relatives in Seama.

Before entering the plaza with a lawn chair in one hand and an umbrella in the other, I detect the delicious scent of "fiesta burgers" being grilled in the food stands and of chili stews cooking in the homes that encircle the plaza.

Soon, two rows of corn-dancers came into the dance arena. Although they are not as elaborately dressed as those of Santo Domingo where the women wear tablitas on their heads, their dance was still a humble request for rain and a good harvest. Women wore the traditional black Pueblo mantas over colorful, long-sleeved dresses. Each manta was tied at the waist with a red, green and black sash. The women carried folded com husks in their white clay-painted hands to gesture with as they danced. Their men partners wore ribbon shirts over Levi pants, and they too were adorned by a sash. A painted gourd rattle carried in each man's right hand was shaken to the accompaniment of drumbeat and singers' chant.

The combination eagle, buffalo and butterfly dance was beautifully performed by the youth of the village. Clad in black shirts and pants three young men honored the buffalo by wearing black-dyed pelts with horns on their heads, while the eagle dancers wore a lifelike head of the revered bird. Brilliantly colored wings on the backs of the girls offered an image of butterflies floating in the field. All dancers wore rust-colored moccasins made by the tribal members.

Clouds that had gathered into a gray formation were now producing the tap tap sound of rain on my blue umbrella. Soon, flashes of lightning pranced across the darkening skies, and thunder shook the earth. Torrential rain come quickly for several minutes, then turned into a gentle shower.

Dust vanished, cool fresh moist air was present, and Governor of Laguna Pueblo, Roland Johnson, was speaking in our Keresan language. In fervent tones he thanked the dancers and the spectators for participating in this day of celebration. Shortly, the procession led by a Catholic Franciscan friar would return the statue of St. Ann to the church. The arbor in which she had sat all day would be dismantled.

For me, the time to feast was at hand. Red chili posole, green chili stew, lamb ribs, bread baked in an outdoor oven, and homemade pies greeted me at cousin Molly's home. The visit was all too short. I had to return to Albuquerque before darkness came.

As I headed east on Interstate-40, a fantastic rainbow arched over the mesas. It gave me sudden cause to thank the Great Spirit for a truly blessed day.

—*Pueblo Horizons*, Fall 1998.

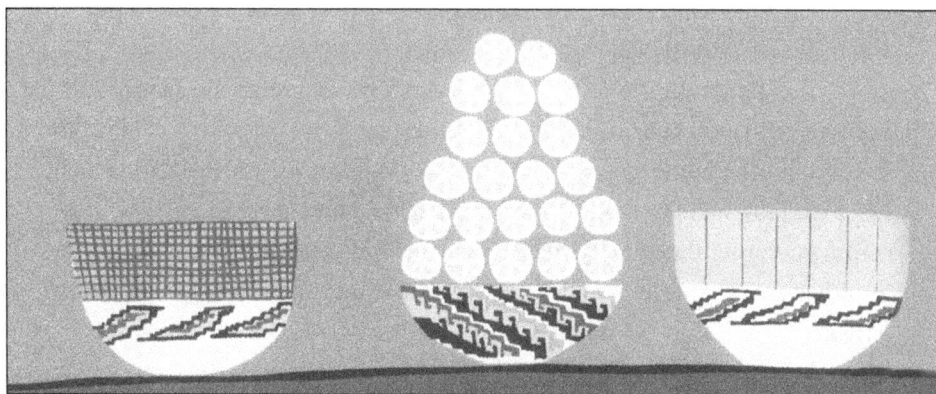

Feasting bowls.

The Taos Pow-Wow

"The earth does not belong to man, man belongs to the earth. All things are connected, like the blood that unites one family. This we know."

—Chief Seattle

The coffee boils in the large gray enamel-coated coffee pot, which rests on a wire grill over the glowing red embers of the dying fire. Soon it will give us the rich aromatic brew to go with our meal of fry bread and of the stew made with elk meat and chicos, the dry roasted corn now plump and sweet in the soup. My friends and I are at an American Indian encampment.

From the highway, the Plains Indians' tepees are visible before the canvas tents, the RVs, the pick-up trucks, and the tree branch sculptured shelters that sit on the grass-covered field on the Taos Pueblo reservation. Here camp life is lived in true Indian style, even to cooking and eating out of doors after the manner of their ancestors thousands of years ago. Below the majestic Taos Mountain, in whose inner sanctum lies the sacred Blue Lake, these First Americans come from far and near each second weekend in July to renew old friendships and to make new ones.

Tua-Tah, meaning" our village" in the Tiwa tongue of the Taos people, has survived 1,000 years through invasions by the Spaniards, the 1680 Pueblo Revolt, and the battle against the United States government in 1847, which left 250 Taos Indians dead. Today the Pueblo hosts the annual Pow-Wow commemorating the old days when Taos was well known as a trading center for other tribes, as well as Mexicans, mountain men, and the new American settlers.

A circular arbor of tree branches and leaves surrounds the dance arena constructed by the Taos Pueblo men several days before the event. A speaker's stand has been built for announcing the program. One notes that this is an authentic Pow-Wow: it has all the natural elements for dancing, feet placed directly on Mother Earth with Father Sky looking down. Within the arena's circle the ancient faith is relived through the songs and rhythmic movements of a people called The American Indian.

Intricate designs of multicolored beads decorate the full length buckskin dresses worn by the women. Jingle dresses with metal cones clatter as the agile teenage girls walk about the grounds with their friends. Bright-colored shawls with long fringes are seen everywhere, on myself and on women who will dance. The children are garbed in their tribal dress, waiting impatiently for the dances to begin. As part of the costume the men have painted their faces, and sport flamboyant roaches made of deer tails or porcupine hair atop their heads. Colorful bustles have been secured to dancers' backs for the fancy-dance contests. Beaded moccasins are the footwear for the celebration. Shell, bone, porcupine quills, bright ribbons, and yarn make elaborate outfits for the performers. All contestants come dancing into the arena at grand entry time twice a day, at noon and in the evening. As the high pitch of the lead Singer begins, the other drum group members follow in songs, first to the American flag, then to the sun and the rain to the great buffalo and all the other animals in the forest, to the sacred land and its people. The dancing has begun; let there be spiritual awareness all around us.

—*Pueblo Horizons*, Summer 1996.

Offerings to all.

About the Author

Katherine Acoya Augustine was born on September 30 1929, in Paguate Village on the Laguna Pueblo Reservation in New Mexico She went to school at the Paguate Day School from 1935–1942, Albuquerque Indian High School 1942–1947, Sage Memorial Hospital School of Nursing, Ganado, Arizona for a Registered Nurse diploma 1947–1950, and the University of Arizona in Tucson, Nursing Leadership training program in 1960–1961.

Her first job as a nurse was at the Indian Health Service Hospital, Fort Defiance Arizona, 1950–1951, followed by nursing at the Women's and Children's Hospital, 1951–1953 Albuquerque, and retiring from nursing at the New Mexico, Presbyterian Hospital Center, 1954–1983. In her career she worked as a Staff Nurse, Head Nurse, and Nurse Educator Supervisor with a specialty in Intravenous Therapy. She also taught throughout New Mexico in the hospitals that were under management by the Presbyterian Hospital. After retirement she worked for the Indian Health Service at the Acoma-CanoncitoLaguna Hospital in San Fidel and the Albuquerque Indian Hospital as a Clinical Nurse, retiring a second time after nine years in 1993.

Her travels include teaching Intravenous Therapy at the invitation of People to People International Citizen Ambassador Program in five cities in the People's Republic of China 1983, as well as in Moscow St. Petersburg and Siberia Russia and Central Asia (Uzbekistan) October 1991, at Vilnius University Hospital in Lithuania October 1992. Other travels included trips to the Sister Cities of Albuquerque; Sasebo, Japan and cities in Japan in 1979, 1981, 1986, 1997, Helmstedt, Germany 1989, 1996, 2000, Hnalien, Taiwan 1986, and Guadalajara, Mexico in 1987. For the Friendship Force of New Mexico she traveled to Seoul, South Korea 1979, Manila, Philippines, Hong Kong 1982, Australia and New Zealand 1994, the Tarahumara Indian Country, Mexico 1969, 1981, 1984, as well as to Eastern and Western Europe including Berlin and Czechoslovakia.

Community involvement has included being a volunteer at the Indian Pueblo Cultural Center (IPCC), and the Chair of Education for the IPCC

Friends Board 1995–1998. She wrote for the IPCC newsletter *Pueblo Horizons* and worked on the committee of the Ancient Living Village. She as served as a Health Board member for the Acoma-Canoncito-Laguna Hospital, was vice-president, of the Laguna Colony of Albuquerque, worked on committees updating bylaws and education assistance for Colony members. As a Vice-President in 2001 of the Senior Arts Board she worked to develop a video, *The Art of Aging*. She was an active member of the Albuquerque Sister Cities Foundation Board, serving as its 2nd Vice-President, and was on the Diabetes Education Committee at the Albuquerque Indian Hospital. Her nursing experience lead to involvement with the Environmental Health Community Advisory Committee, a University of New Mexico Research project regarding environmental health issues in Native American communities. She also served on the Council of Elders through the New Mexico Geriatric Education Center for improvement of health care of New Mexico American Indian elders that included education and training of health care providers. With Dick Knipfing of Albuquerque Channel 13 TV she helped promote America-Japan Week 1995 by hosting Japanese visitors. For twenty-three years she volunteered as chase crew member at the Albuquerque International Hot Air Balloon Fiesta. She was on the Advisory Committee of the Southwest Repertory Theatre production of *The Indolent Boys* in 2002. She was a volunteer at the Children's Art Exhibit at the New Mexico Arts and Crafts Fair each June for seven years.

Katherine has been a member of numerous organizations including the People to People International Citizen Ambassador Program, American Intravenous Nurses Society, Friendship Force of New Mexico, Albuquerque Sister Cities, Natural History Museum, Highland Pen People, Southwest Writers Workshop, Friends of the Indian Pueblo Cultural Center, Laguna Pueblo and Laguna Colony of Albuquerque, New Mexico, Martin Luther King Day Council and the Albuquerque Human Rights Board, Albuquerque, New Mexico.

Katherine received an International Human Right Award under the auspices of the United Nations for ambassadorship around the world. She is in Who's Who in American Nursing 1984. Other awards she has received include a Bronze metal and ceremonial sash from the people of Lithuania

1992, Certificate of Appreciation for contribution to Science and Technology from the People's Republic of China 1983, as well as certificates of appreciation from the Army Corps of Engineers, Albuquerque Public Schools and International Balloon Fiesta. In 2001 she was inducted into the Senior Hall of Fame and was invited to be on a panel of Native American Women Journalists in March 2002. Later that same year she was named a Nursing Legend for contributions to the nursing profession in New Mexico and abroad by the New Mexico Hospitals and Health Systems Association and the March of Dimes. The following year, 2003, she was awarded American Native Woman of the Year by the Indian Pueblo Cultural Center and the New Mexico Commission on the Status of Women for contributions to the Native American heritage by way of culture, community and world health. A feature article was written about her in *New Mexico Magazine*, November 2004. The next year she received a Certificate of Appreciation from the University of New Mexico Medical School for teaching medical students.

Katherine is included in the Albuquerque Museum of Art and Culture 2016 exhibits on the Albuquerque Indian School and Exhibit on Spirituality and in a video *The Women on the Mother Road in New Mexico*, Assertion Films, Los Angeles, California, October 2016.

She has published many articles in the *Senior Times Newspaper* 1995–1996, *Pueblo Horizons* 1995–2001, *Prime Time Newspaper, Storyteller*, Newsletters for Sister Cities of Albuquerque, New Mexico Friendship Force, the New Mexico Geriatric Education Center, as well as for the *Albuquerque Tribune* and *Round the Roundhouse* Newspapers. She coauthored *Living in an Indian Pueblo Today*, a textbook publication for children seven to nine years old, November 1999. Katherine has been a luncheon speaker at the Southwest Writer's conference and presenter of a program on *Finding the Details that Bring Your Travel Writing to Life*, September 2002. She wrote a short personal biography, *Breaking Molds*, in November 2002 and an article *Christmas Eve at My Pueblo*, December 2002, both for *New Mexico Magazine*.

www.ingramcontent.com/pod-product-compliance
Lightning Source LLC
Chambersburg PA
CBHW021534270326
41930CB00008B/1254